Wicked SPANISH

BY HOWARD TOMB

WORKMAN PUBLISHING • NEW YORK

ACKNOWLEDGMENTS

Many thanks to Jorge Aizenman and Marcella Villanueva for their painstaking translating work, and to Shawna McCarthy, Sally Kovalchick, Patty Brown, John Boswell, and Ben Stoner.

Library of Congress Cataloging-in-Publication Data
Tomb, Howard
Wicked Spanish/by Howard Tomb
p. cm.
ISBN 0-89480-861-3
1. Spanish language—conversation and phrase books—Humor. 2. Mexico—Description and travel—1981—Guide-books—Humor. 3. Latin America—Description and travel—1981—Humor. 4. Spain—Description and travel—1981—Guide-books—Humor. I. Title.
PN6231.S646T6 1991
468.3'421'0207—dc20 90-20799 CIP

Illustrations by Jared Lee
Cover and book design by Paul Hanson
Cover photograph by Super Stock

Workman books are available at special discounts when purchased in bulk for premiums and sales promotions as well as for fund-raising or educational use. Special editions or book excerpts can also be created to specification. For details, contact the Special Sales Director at the address below.

Workman Publishing, 708 Broadway, New York, NY 10003

Printed in the United States of America
First printing March 1991
20 19 18 17 16 15 14 13 12

CONTENTS

BIENVENIDO

Travel in Spanish-speaking countries means more than cheap hotels and quick suntans—one must adapt to foreign customs and attitudes. To the un-initiated, Hispanic culture can be confusing and frustrating.

Our forms of logic, efficiency, and refrigeration are largely unknown. Other things we take for granted are rare or nonexistent, including clearly marked prices, paved roads, and college-educated waitresses.

We may be startled by pigs as they run through the streets or hang over the sidewalk. We may be terrified by blind taxi drivers. We may be confused when locals fail to respond to wads of cash waved in the air.

Naïve, unprepared travelers feel angry and humiliated. But Wicked Travelers never seem to suffer. They are always relaxed. They have an intuitive understanding of life abroad and a special sensitivity for alien cultures and ideas. They are also heavily armed. Not with gold cards, loud voices, or idle threats in English, but with warm smiles, patient attitudes, and a variety of verbal weapons that natives understand.

GETTING AROUND 🚕

THE OLD MAN AND THE CHEVY

The mañana concept is a paradox of Hispanic culture. While the clerks and waiters of an entire nation may appear to be in a collective coma, the taxi drivers seem to have Benzedrine in their blood.

The antiquity of many taxis only adds to the terror of high-speed rides. But before you resort to violence or leap from the vehicle, try a little verbal persuasion.

This car is amazing.	*Este carro es increíble.*	*ES-tay CA-roh ehs in-kray-EE-blay.*
I never knew chicken wire had so many uses.	*Yo no sabía que la tela metálica tenía tantos usos.*	*Yoh noh sah-BEE-ah kay la TAY-la meh-TAH-lee-kah ten-EE-ah TAHN-tohs OOS-ohs.*
When did the brakes go out?	*¿Cuándo se fueron los frenos?*	*KWAN-doh say fooEH-ron los FREH-nohs?*
In the Eisenhower years?	*¿En la época de Carranza?*	*En la ay-POH-kah day cah-RONZ-ah?*
Please give us helmets/ blindfolds.	*Por favor dénos cascos/unas vendas para los ojos.*	*Pohr fah-VOAR DAY-nohs KAHS-kohs/OON-ahs VAIN-das PAH-rah los OH-hoes.*

🚗 **GETTING AROUND**

Look, if you don't slow down, I won't pay you.	*Mire, si no reduce la velocidad, no le voy a pagar.*	*MEER-ay, see noh reh-doo-seh la vay-LO-see-DOD, noh leh voee ah pah-gahr.*
That's much better, thanks.	*Mucho mejor, gracias.*	*MOO-cho meh-HORE, GRAH-see-ahs.*

DISCLAIMER OF WICKEDNESS

In consideration of 1) the explosive tempers engendered by the combined effects of hot weather, hotter food, and the Laws of Machismo, and 2) the insensitivity of certain Americans abroad, combined with said travelers' wrenching pronunciation and deeply mistaken sense of invulnerability, the author and his assigns, agents, bodyguards, pallbearers and heirs hereby disclaim, categorically deny and strangle at birth all claims and actions arising from the use, misuse, or failure to use any of the words, phrases, strategies, or attitudes contained in this volume.

GETTING AROUND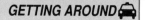

STOP BUS!

Buses are great travel bargains. For seventeen cents you can go twenty miles and feel like you've gone two hundred.

Oxygen may be scarce inside; either find a window seat or join the economy-class passengers clinging to the colorfully painted exterior of the vehicle.

Memorize these basic bus-travel phrases.

Yours is the prettiest piglet, miss.	*Su cochinito es el más lindo, señorita.*	*Soo co-chee-NEE-toh ehs el mahs LEEN-doh, SEE-nyoh-REE-tah.*
But it has shat in my lap.	*Pero se me ha cagado en las piernas.*	*PAIR-oh say meh ha cah-GAH-doh en lahs pee-AIR-nahs.*
The cliffs are very steep.	*Los acantilados son muy empinados.*	*Los ah-kan-tee-LA-dohs sohn moo-EE em-pee-nah-dos.*
The bus is very fast.	*El camión es muy rápido.*	*El cam-YONE ehs moo-EE RAH-pee-doh.*
Do I smell an old enchilada?	*¿Acaso huelo una enchilada vieja?*	*Ah-CAH-soh WHAY-loh OO-nah EN-chee-LAH-dah vee-AY-ha?*

| I don't feel well. | *No me siento bien.* | *No may see-EN-toh bee-EN.* |
| Please lend me your hat. | *Por favor présteme su sombrero.* | *Pohr fah-VOAR PRES-tah-may soo som-BRAY-roh.* |

PRAYER OF THE LOST LUGGAGE

O mighty Zapoletoltecoaxacoatlototoc, God of Flight, Locusts and Lost Luggage, please return to me my handsome Gucci bag that went to Guadalajara or Guadalupe. I dare not make a pilgrimage to your Holy Rockpile without the brand-new matching outfit from Bergdorf's contained in said Gucci bag. And if you can spare a moment from your busy schedule, O Winged Reptilian Unhappiness, please firmly smite all cruel and inept baggage handlers.

O poderoso Zapoletoltecoaxacoatlototoc, Dios de la Aviación, Langostas y Equipaje Perdido, por favor a regrésame mi elegante maleta Gucci que fue a parar a Guadalajara o Guadalupe. No me atrevo a hacer un peregrinaje a tu santo montón de piedras sin mi nuevo traje de Bergdorf's contenido dentro de tal maleta Gucci. Y si pudieras darme un minuto de tu valioso tiempo, O Infelicidad Reptilia y Alada, por favor castiga severamente a todo cruel e inepto maletero.

GETTING AROUND 🚕

ADDRESSING THE MULE

If you are ever required to ride a mule or burro, you should have the satisfaction of addressing it in its own tongue. Keep in mind, however, that while all pack animals understand Spanish, none follow directions.

Sweetheart. Darling. Move!	*Cariño. Querida. ¡Muévete!*	*Cah-REE-nyoh. Kay-REE-dah. MWAIVE-ay-tay!*
I'm talking to you.	*Te estoy hablando.*	*Tay ess-TOY ah-BLAHN-doh.*
I've seen turds more energetic than you!	*¡Yo he visto mojones más enérgicos que tú!*	*Yoh ay VEES-toh moh-HOH-nehs mahs eh-NEHR-hee-kohs kay too!*
And I've had enough of your noisy complaints!	*¡Y ya basta de tus quejas escandalosas!*	*Ee yah BAHS-tah day toos KAY-hahs ehs-kahn-dah-LOH-sahs!*
I will not negotiate.	*No negociaré.*	*No nay-GOH-see-ah-RAY.*
Shall I beat you to within an inch of your life?	*¿Acaso quieres que te dé una paliza hasta el borde de la muerte?*	*Ah-KAH-soh kee-AIR-ace kay tay day OO-nah pah-LEE-zah AHS-tah el BOR-day la MWER-tay?*

🚕 *GETTING AROUND*

| Whoa! I said whoa! Pretty please, whoa! | ¡Alto! ¡Dije alto! ¡Por favorcito, alto! | *AHL-toh! DEE-hay AHL-toh! Pohr fah-voar-SEE-toh AHL-toh!* |

CUSTOMS TIPS

The wide variety of contraband available south of the border provides jobs for thousands of U.S. Customs agents. They don't necessarily want to arrest you, but they are trusted to protect the border. And they love to slap handcuffs on smugglers and left-wing liberals. Adjusting your appearance may speed your border crossing.

BAD	BETTER	BEST
Surfboard	Sailboard	Tennis racquet
Huraches	Reeboks	Loafers
Drawstring Pants	Jeans	Starched chinos
Tie-dyed T-shirt	Polo shirt	Brooks Brothers' button-down
Sunglasses	No glasses	Thick glasses
Volkswagen van	Dodge mini-van	Forty-foot RV
Old Volvo	New Buick	New Volvo

GETTING AROUND 🚗

TIPPING POLICEMEN

When Mexico City's chief of police was asked how he could build a $2.5 million mansion on his $65 a week salary, he said he saved carefully and made wise investments. He didn't mention the tradition of *la mordida*, "the little bite."

Any visitor driving a car is likely to get bitten, but a "tip" will not always free one from the jaws of injustice. Some policemen want to accept money *and* preserve their honor.

What seems to be the problem, officer?	*¿Cuál es el problema, oficial?*	*Kwal ehs ehl pro-BLEH-mah, oh-fee-si-AL?*
The light was quite green, actually.	*En realidad, el semáforo estaba en verde.*	*En ray-AL-ee-DAHD, el seh-MAH-fo-roh ehs-TAH-bah ehn VAIR-day.*
No, I am not calling you a liar.	*No, yo no lo estoy llamando mentiroso.*	*No, yoh no lo ess-TOY yah-MAHN-doh men-tee-ROH-soh.*
I'm sure we can work this out.	*Estoy seguro que podemos arreglar esto.*	*Ess-TOY say-GOO-roh kay poh-DEH-mohs ah-re-GLAHR EHS-toh.*

🚕 *GETTING AROUND*

Here are my papers.	*Aquí están mis papeles.*	*Ah-KEE es-TAHN meece pah-PEH-lehs.*
Would these green papers help?	*¿Servirían también estos papelitos verdes?*	*Sair-vee-REE-ahn tahm-bee-EN EHS-tohs PAH-peh-lee-tohs VAIR-dehs?*
Do you need so many of them?	*¿Acaso necesita tantos?*	*Ah-CAH-so nay-say-SEE-tah TAHN-tos?*
Do the handcuffs have to be so tight?	*¿Tienen que estar tan apretadas las esposas?*	*Tee-EH-nen kay ess-ṬAR tahn ah-pray-TAH-dahs las ess-POH-sahs?*

GETTING AROUND 🚕

PEDESTRIAN ADVISORY

Local drivers will display behavior different from what you're used to at home. The chart below shows typical Latino driving speeds under assorted conditions.

TERRAIN	PREFERRED SPEED	
	MPH	KPH
Thick Jungle	50	80
High Brush	55	90
Rabbit Trail	65	105
Footpath	70	110
Cliff Edge in Thunderstorm	95	155
Sidewalk	100	160
Super Highway	110	175
Paved Super Highway	55	90
City Street	15	25

Note: No driver will slow for red lights or oncoming vehicles, lest he be considered weak and feminine.

 GETTING AROUND

ASSORTED ROAD SIGNS

If you must drive, memorize the road signs unique
to Spanish-speaking countries.

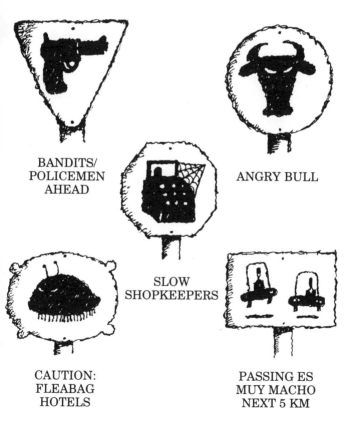

BANDITS/
POLICEMEN
AHEAD

ANGRY BULL

SLOW
SHOPKEEPERS

CAUTION:
FLEABAG
HOTELS

PASSING ES
MUY MACHO
NEXT 5 KM

DESTINATIONS 🏨

SURVIVING THE HOTEL

Old hotels—and that includes most of them—may have a wide variety of rooms, ranging from revolting to barely adequate. Never check into a hotel before looking at the room you are to be given. And don't rely on a guidebook for the nightly rate; inflation can raise prices in a matter of hours.

Could I see a couple of rooms, please?	¿Podría ver un par de cuartos por favor?	*Poh-DREE-ah vair oon par day KWAR-tohs pohr fah-VOAR?*
I understand this building is 400 years old.	Entiendo que este edificio tiene cuatrocientos años.	*En-tee-EN-doh kay EHS-tay eh-dee-FEECE-ee-yoh tee-EN-ay KWAH-troh-see-EN-tohs AHN-yohs.*
Is that the original paint/maid?	¿Es esta la pintura/sirvienta original?	*Ehs EHS-tah lah peen-TOO-rah / seer-VEE-ehn-tah oh-REE-jeen-nahl?*
How authentic!	¡Qué auténtico!	*Kay ow-TEN-tee-koh!*

DESTINATIONS

I don't mind the spiders much.	*No me molestan tanto las arañas.*	*No may moh-LES-tahn TAHN-toh las ah-RAHN-yahs.*
But I'd prefer a room without scorpions.	*Pero preferiría una habitación sin alacranes.*	*PAIR-oh PRAY-fair-eer-REE-ah OO-nah ah-bee-tah-see-OHN seen ah-lah-KRAH-nehss.*
Is there a room that doesn't face the bus station/ mescal bar/ slaughterhouse?	*¿Tiene alguna habitación que no dé a la estación de camiones/cantina/matadero?*	*Tee-EH-nay ahl-GOO-nah ah-bee-tah-see-OHN kay no DAY ah la ehs-tah-see-OHN day kah-mee-OH-nayss/cahn-TEE-nah/mah-tah-DARE-oh?*
Is there a room with a window/ bathroom?	*¿Tiene alguna habitación con ventana/baño?*	*Tee-EH-nay ahl-GOO-nah ah-bee-tah-see-OHN con ven-TAH-nah/BAHN-yoh?*
Is there another hotel in this town?	*¿Hay otro hotel en esta ciudad?*	*AH-ee OH-troh oh-TEL en EHS-tah see-oo-DAHD?*

DESTINATIONS

WHEN IN RUINS

A trip to Mexico or Peru wouldn't be complete without a visit to ancient ruins.

If you want to hire a guide, interview several candidates before selecting one. Many historical facts have been lost; look for a guide with a vivid imagination.

If your Spanish isn't very good, you may want to test candidates by asking these questions in English.

Who is depicted in that carving?	*¿Quién está representado en ese grabado?*	*Kee-EN es-TAH rep-ray-zen-TAH-doh en EH-say grah-BAH-doh?*
What happened to his heart/head/genitals?	*¿Qué pasó con su corazón/cabeza/órganos?*	*Kay pah-SOH kohn soo coh-rah-ZOHN/cah-BAYS-ah/OR-gah-nohs?*
My friend, you are a sick man.	*Amigo, usted está mal de la cabeza.*	*Ah-MEE-goh, oos-TED ehs-TAH mahl day la cah-BAY-sah.*
You're hired.	*Queda contratado.*	*KAY-dah kohn-trah-TAH-doh.*

UNDERSTANDING ZAPOTEC BASKETBALL

Visiting ancient sites is more enjoyable when you know their history. Small stadiums are central features of many Mexican ruins, and as your guide will explain, a sport like basketball was played there. Here are a few details about the game.

HOW POINTS WERE SCORED
One Point: Putting Ball Through Hoop, Holding, Shoving
Two Points: Clubbing, Stabbing, Blinding
Three Points: Dismembering, Disemboweling, Decapitating

FAVORITE TEAMS OF THE SMALL TEN
- Gourd Valley College Rain Gods
- Feathered Serpent School High Priests
- Primitive State Cougar-Catchers
- Jungle University Poisonous Mushrooms

NECESSARY EQUIPMENT
- Obsidian Knives
- Feather Shields
- Granite Balls
- Coffins

THE PLAYERS
Average Height: Four feet, four inches
Average Weight: 90 pounds
Average Length of Career: Six minutes

DESTINATIONS

CONFESSION

A town's finest architecture, painting and sculpture are often found at the cathedral. Best of all, the thick stone walls provide natural air-conditioning on hot afternoons.

Forgive me, Father.	*Perdóneme, Padre.*	*Pair-DOH-nay-may, PAH-dray.*
I have never confessed before in my life.	*Nunca me he confesado antes en mi vida.*	*NOON-ka may eh kohn-feh-SAH-doh AHN-tehss en mee VEE-dah.*
In fact, I don't intend to now.	*Ni tampoco pienso hacerlo ahora.*	*Nee tam-POH-koh pee-EN-soh ah-SAIR-loh ah-OHR-ah.*
I came in here to get out of the sun.	*Entré aquí para resguardarme del sol.*	*Ehn-TRAY ah-KEE PAH-rah ress-GWARD-ahr-may del sol.*
How about those Padres?	*¿Y qué tal los Padres de San Diego?*	*Ee kay tahl los PAH-drays day sahn dee-AY-goh?*
You're right. Their relief pitching is a little weak.	*Tiene razón. Los relevistas están un poco flojos.*	*Tee-EN-ay rah-ZOHN. Los ray-lay-VEES-tahs ehs-TAHN oon POH-koh FLO-hohs.*

Maybe they need a little help from above.	*Quizás necesiten un poco de ayuda del cielo.*	*Kee-ZAHS nay-say-SEE-ten oon POH-koh day ah-YOO-dah del see-AY-loh.*
Shall we pray?	*¿Rezamos?*	*Ray-SAH-mohs?*

DEATH TAKES A HOLIDAY

Mexicans remind themselves of fate and forebears during the Days of the Dead, which begin on Halloween. Families make special altars and honor deceased members with gifts of food, cigarettes and liquor.

On the evening of November 2, people parade in costumes and skulls to the grave-yard for a picnic with dead relatives. Children get skeleton dolls and candy skulls with their names printed on the foreheads. Local artisans will be happy to depict you and your family as you will look after you are dead. Join the colorful ceremonies, but:
- Do not offer to nail anyone's coffin shut;
- Do not consume offerings meant for the dead, tequila in particular;
- Do not make offerings of money or Kaopectate;
- Do not tell dead waiters to hurry up.

DESTINATIONS

FINDING THE MUSEUM

The trouble with Latino museums is finding them. Everyone you ask for directions will want you to see the best parts of town on your way to your destination. You may need to ask for directions several times.

Direct us to the Museum of Fine Arts/ Anthropology.	*Diríjanos al museo de Bellas Artes/Antropología.*	*Dee-REE-hah-nos al moo-SAY-oh day BELL-yahss AR-tays / ahn-troh-poh-loh-HEE-ah.*
Left at the church, left at the plaza and left at the hundred-year-old beggar?	*¿A la izquierda en la iglesia, izquierda en la plaza, y a la izquierda en el limosnero de cien años?*	*Ah la ees-kee-AIR-dah en la ee-GLAY-see-ah, ees-kee-AIR-dah en la PLAH-sah, ee ah la ees-kee-AIR-dah en el lee-mohs-NAY-roh day see-EN AHN-yohs?*
Is there another way?	*¿Hay alguna otra ruta?*	*Eye ahl-GOO-nah OH-trah ROO-tah?*
We've met the beggar several times already.	*Pero si ya pasamos por el limosnero varias veces.*	*PAIR-oh see yah pah-SAH-mohs pohr el lee-mohs-NAY-roh VAH-ree-ahss VEH-says.*

DESTINATIONS

Okay, let me get this straight.	Bueno, permítame que lo entienda.	BWAY-noh, pair-MEE-tah-may kay loh ehn-tee-EN-dah.
Right at the iron gate, right on the paved road, right at the meat market, and right at the fried dough seller.	A la derecha en la reja de hierro, a la derecha en el camino pavimentado, a la derecha en el mercado de carne, y a la derecha en el vendedor de churros.	Ah la dah-RAY-cha en lah RAY-ha day YEH-roh, ah lah da-RAY-cha en el kah-MEE-noh pah-vee-men-TAH-doh, ah la da-RAY-cha en el mair-KAH-doh day CAR-nay, ee ah la da-RAY-cha en el ven-day-DOHR day CHOO-rohs.
Thanks very much. We are sure to find it now.	Muchas gracias. Seguro que lo encontramos ahora.	MOO-chahs GRAH-see-ahs. Say-GOO-roh kay loh en-con-TRAH-mohs ah-oh-ra.

DESTINATIONS

BEACH BLANKET LINGO

The vendors wandering
along Latin American
beaches are not marketing
experts. You can help them
by explaining your needs
as a consumer.

Yes, madam, that is a beautiful wool serape.	*Sí, señora, ése es un lindo serape de lana.*	*See, seen-YOHR-ah, EH-say ehs oon LEEN-doh sah-RAH-pay day LAH-nah.*
The burro motif is appealing.	*El motivo con el burro es interesante.*	*El moh-TEE-voh kohn ehl BOO-roh ehs ehn-tair-eh-SAHN-tay.*
But it is 95 degrees here on the beach.	*Pero hace treinta y cinco grados aquí en la playa.*	*PAIR-oh AH-seh TRAIN-tah ee SEEN-koh GRAH-dos ah-KEY en lah PLAH-yah.*
I do not need 10 pounds of wool today.	*No necesito cuatro kilos de tela de lana hoy.*	*No nay-say-SEE-toh KWAH-troh KEE-lohs day TAY-lah day LAH-nah OH-ee.*
Have you got any cold beer?	*¿Tiene cerveza fría?*	*Tee-EN-ay sair-VAY-sah FREE-ah?*

ATTENTION THIRD-WORLD SHOPPERS

The robust produce and handmade items of the less-industrialized world may seem like bargains. But before buying anything—and especially before bringing it home—consider the hazards.

ITEM	BENEFIT	DRAWBACK
Wooden mask	Looks great in den or playroom.	Tiny insects eat mask, make home in den or playroom.
Sombrero	Authentic replica of actual hat.	Can't be packed; looks ridiculous on plane ride.
Assorted produce	Lots of flavor for pennies a serving.	Rinse in local water may add typhus germs.
Piñata	Bright colors, fun for kids.	Certain to be torn in half at border by customs agents.
Marijuana	Almost free, mind-blowing.	"Making friends" in a sweaty Mexican prison.
Heroin	Super-discount, 95% pure.	Being shot at dawn in a sweaty Mexican prison.

SUSTENANCE

RESTAURANT SURVIVAL TECHNIQUES

It is painful to watch your brief vacation evaporate while waiters and waitresses smoke, chat, hang out, and nap.

They are not trying to irritate you. They merely want to make your meal more delicious. Just before dawn, when the food is served, it will seem like a blessing, no matter how lousy it is. A few phrases may help move things along.

I feel faint!	*¡Me desmayo!*	*May dess-MAI-oh!*
My blood pressure is dropping!	*¡Me está bajando la presión!*	*May ehs-TAH bah-HAN-doh lah preh-see-YOHN!*
Help! Emergency!	*¡Socorro! ¡Emergencia!*	*Soh-KOH-rroh! Eh-mair-HEN-see-ah!*
Is there a waiter in the house?	*¿Hay un mesero aquí?*	*Ay oon may-SARE-oh ah-KEE?*
Are you a waiter/ waitress? Thank God!	*¿Es usted un/ una mesero/ mesera? ¡Gracias a Dios!*	*Ehs oos-TED oon/oon-ah may-SARE-oh/may-SARE-ah? GRAH-see-ahs ah DEE-ohs!*

Forget the menu!	*¡Olvídese de la carta!*	*Ole-VEE-day-say day la CAR-tah!*
Just show me to your kitchen.	*Sólo muéstreme su cocina.*	*So-loh MWAY-stray-may soo koh-SEE-nah.*
I'll help myself.	*Me sirvo solo.*	*May SEER-voh so-loh.*
But you might as well take my breakfast order now.	*Más vale que tome mi orden del desayuno ahora.*	*Mass VAH-lay kay TOH-may mee OR-den del des-seye-OO-noh ah-OR-ah.*

SUSTENANCE

LOOK OUT FOR "CHICKEN OF THE TREES"

Latin cuisine includes hundreds of unusual dishes, but visitors may not want to taste them all. "Chicken of the trees," for example, is an iguana. Still, there is sure to be something nourishing and bland on the menu. Learn how to ask for it by name.

What lies motionless under the spicy chocolate sauce?	*¿Qué yace immóvil dentro del mole?*	*Kay YAH-say imm-MOH-veel DEN-troh del MOH-lay?*
What oozes from the depths of the stuffed pepper?	*¿Qué emana de las profundidades del chile relleno?*	*Kay ay-MAH-nah day las proh-foon-dee-DAH-days del CHEE-lay ray-YAY-noh?*
What stares at me with glassy eyes?	*¿Qué es lo que me mira con ojos vidriosos?*	*Kay ehs loh kay may MEER-ah con OH-hohs vee-dree-OH-sohs?*
Ah. I had that last night.	*Ah. Comí eso anoche.*	*Ah. Coh-MEE EH-soh ah-NOH-chay.*

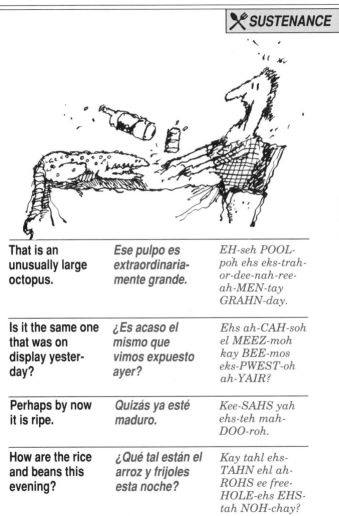

That is an unusually large octopus.	*Ese pulpo es extraordinaria-mente grande.*	*EH-seh POOL-poh ehs eks-trah-or-dee-nah-ree-ah-MEN-tay GRAHN-day.*
Is it the same one that was on display yesterday?	*¿Es acaso el mismo que vimos expuesto ayer?*	*Ehs ah-CAH-soh el MEEZ-moh kay BEE-mos eks-PWEST-oh ah-YAIR?*
Perhaps by now it is ripe.	*Quizás ya esté maduro.*	*Kee-SAHS yah ehs-teh mah-DOO-roh.*
How are the rice and beans this evening?	*¿Qué tal están el arroz y frijoles esta noche?*	*Kay tahl ehs-TAHN ehl ah-ROHS ee free-HOLE-ehs EHS-tah NOH-chay?*

SUSTENANCE ✗

GUIDE TO PAINLESS DINING

Contrary to popular belief, extremely hot foods are
not good for you. That is why they hurt so much.
People who like to dine in pain will enjoy eating in
Mexico. But those who prefer non-toxic dishes will
also find appealing items on any menu.

I love hot food.	*Me encanta la comida picante.*	*May en-KAHN-tah la koh-MEE-dah pee-KAHN-tay.*
But I ate a serrano pepper last week.	*Pero comí un chile serrano la semana pasada.*	*PAIR-oh coh-MEE oon CHEE-lay sair-AH-noh la say-MAH-nah pah-SAH-dah.*
It really opened my eyes!	*¡En verdad me abrió los ojos!*	*En vair-DAD may ah-bree-OH los OH-hohs!*
And it lost none of its potency passing through my body.	*Y no perdidó nada de su potencia al pasar por mi organismo.*	*Ee no pair-dee-DOH NAH-dah day soo poh-TEN-see-ah ahl pah-SAR pohr mee or-gah-NEEZ-moh.*
The swelling is going down now.	*La hinchazón ya se me está pasando.*	*La EEN-cha-sohn yaa say may ehs-TAH pah-SAHN-doh.*

✗ SUSTENANCE

The blisters will heal soon.	*Las ampollas se curarán pronto.*	*Las ahm-POLL-yahs say KOO-rah-RAHN PROHN-toh.*
But for now, dry toast will be fine.	*Pero por ahora, pan tostado sin mantequilla.*	*PAIR-oh pohr ah-OR-ah, pahn toss-TAH-doh seen MAN-tay-KEE-ah.*

PRAYER OF THE LARGE INTESTINE

O Saint Elena the Rather Plump, I beg your favor to punish and kill the Devils that have taken adverse possession of my normally rugged digestive system. And, O Thunder Thighs, I have lost fifteen pounds in the last three days and would be willing to make a special pilgrimage every year to your shrine in Cancún if I do not gain this weight back, your Holy Circumference.

O Santa Elena la Regordeta, te ruego el favor de castigar y matar a los Diabólicos que se han apoderado adversamente de mi normalmente sano aparato digestivo. Y, O Piernas Estruendosas, he perdido siete kilos en los últimos tres días y estaré dispuesto(a) a hacer un peregrinaje especial cada año a tu templo en Cancún si no recupero estos kilos de nuevo, O Bendita Circunferencia.

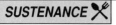

THE MEN-ONLY BAR

On a hot afternoon, few things satisfy like a cold *cerveza* and a few handfuls of salty chips. Unfortunately, many drinking establishments are for men only. The few women in such places are assumed to be for hire. A general announcement may be required to avoid misunderstanding and injury.

Excuse me, gentlemen!	*¡Discúlpenme, caballeros!*	*Dees-KOOL-pen-may, CAH-bah-YAIR-ohs!*
I'd like to make an announcement.	*Me gustaría hacer un anuncio.*	*May goos-tah-REE-ah ah-SAIR oon ah-NOON-see-oh.*
This is my wife.	*Esta es mi esposa.*	*EHS-tah ehs mee ess-POH-sah.*
She is from a good family.	*Es de buena familia.*	*Ehs day BWAY-nah fah-MEEL-ee-ah.*
Do not stare at her.	*No la miren.*	*No lah MEE-ren.*
Do not touch her.	*No la toquen.*	*No lah TOH-ken.*
We are here for the beer.	*Estamos aquí por la cerveza.*	*Ehs-TAH-mohs ah-KEE pohr la sair-VAY-sah.*

FOR WOMEN ONLY: COIN-A-CURSE

A lone woman may be the object of rude comments from Spanish-speaking men. The best response is silence, but some victims insist on counter-attack.

Create your own invective from the columns below. Adjectives follow nouns. Begin with a word from column C and add words from A and B, as in *rata de al cantarilla incontinente sin dientes* (toothless incontinent sewer rat).

A	B	C
filthy *cochino* co-CHEE-noh	**polyester-clad** *revestido en poliester* reh-VEHS-tee-doh ehn POH-lee-ES-tair	**butcher boy** *niño carnicero* NEEN-yoh CAR-nee-SAY-roh
toothless *sin dientes* seen dee-EN-tays	**incontinent** *incontinente* in-CON-teen-EN-tay	**sewer rat** *rata de al cantarilla* RA-tah day al KAN-tah-ree-yah
cretinous *cretino* cray-TEE-noh	**ill-bred** *malnacido* mahl-nah-SEED-oh	**maggot-mouth** *boca de gusano* BOH-kah day goo-SAH-noh
squirming *retorcido* ray-TOHR-see-doh	**frog-lipped** *labios de sapo* LAH-bee-ohs deh SAH-poh	**midget** *enano* ay-NOH-noh

Note: Men who value their lives should never utter these phrases.

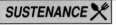

SUSTENANCE

DRINKING TO KILL
THE CRITTERS WITHIN

Try to drink only bottled fluids. If you consume tap water, perhaps on your toothbrush or in the form of ice, you'll have to modify your drinking habits even further.

Bartender! A Pepto Bismol, straight up!	*¡Barman! ¡Un Pepto Bismol solo!*	*BAHR-mahn! Oon PEHP-toh BEEZ-mahl so-loh!*
I am very grateful. And now, a toast!	*Se lo agradezco mucho. ¡Y ahora un brindis!*	*Say loh ah-grah-DAYS-koh MOO-choh. Ee ah-OR-ah oon brin-DEES!*
To the eternal suffering of a certain restaurateur!	*¡Al eterno sufrimiento de cierto dueño de restaurante!*	*Ahl ay-TARE-noh soo-free-mee-EN-toh day see-AIR-toh DWAIN-yoh day res-taw-RAHN-tay!*
May large armadillos copulate in his colon!	*¡Ojalá que enormes armadillos copulen en sus intestinos!*	*Oh-hah-LAH kay ay-NOR-mays AR-mah-DEEL-yohs koh-poo-len een sus in-tes-TEE-nohs!*

May flames shoot from between his cheeks!	*¡Ojalá que dispare llamas por el culo!*	*Oh-hah-LAH kay diss-PAH-ray YAH-mahs pohr ehl koo-loh!*
May he eat his own cooking and croak!	*¡Ojalá que coma su propia comida y muera!*	*Oh-hah-LAH kay COH-mah soo PRO-pee-ah koh-MEE-dah ee MWARE-ah!*

MEXICAN DRINKS OF DEATH

Tequila is a potent liquor made from cactus. It tastes so awful that many people lick salt and suck on a lime after each swallow. The more obscure brands of tequila should be sipped through your clenched teeth, carefully straining out the sand, twigs, and insect parts.

Mescal is a mildly hallucinogenic liquor also made from cactus. It adds a fresh, unpredictable element to any drunken afternoon. If drinking mescal fails to make you violently ill, try chewing on the dead worm at the bottom of your bottle.

Pulque is made by *pulqueños* who chew on cactus, spit into a jar and let the mixture sit for a few weeks. Beer is okay for some people, but it takes a real man to drink a warm glass of fermented Mexican spit.

SUSTENANCE ✖️

MOCTEZUMA'S MEDICAL EMERGENCY

No matter how careful you are, you will probably get sick during your visit. When the agony overtakes you, there are two things to remember: 1) Nobody lives forever; 2) Local doctors will do everything in their power to make your last hours on earth as painful and unpleasant as possible.

I ate/drank something in your country.	*Comí/bebí algo en su país.*	*Coh-MEE / bay-BEE AHL-goh en soo pah-EES.*
Please call a priest/ travel agent.	*Por favor llame a un cura/agente de viajes.*	*Pohr fah-VOAR YAH-may ah oon COO-rah / ah-HEN-tay day vee-AH-hays.*
I would like to make a will/ receive last rites.	*Me gustaría hacer un testamento/ recibir extre-maunción.*	*May goos-tah-REE-ah ah-SER oon tes-tah-MEN-toh / reh-see-BEER ehs-tray-mah-oon-see-OHN.*
Please send my body home on the next flight.	*Por favor, manden mi cadáver a casa en el próximo vuelo.*	*Pohr fah-VOAR , MAN-den mee kah-DAH-ver ah CAH-sah en el PROHK-see-moh VWAY-loh.*

SUSTENANCE

EAT AND RUN

One of the pleasures of Latino life is snacking at a street vendor's stand. If the meat you order is boiling in oil, many of the bacteria and parasites will be dead by the time they hit your plate. If you avoid garnishes, you may survive the meal.

Good day, sir. What is that?	*Buen día señor. ¿Qué es eso?*	*Bwain DEE-ah seen-yohr. Kay ehs EH-soh?*
I can see it is meat.	*Veo que es carne.*	*VAY-oh kay ehs CAR-nay.*
But what species?	*¿Pero de qué tipo?*	*PAIR-oh day kay TEE-poh?*
I can't find that in my dictionary.	*No encuentro eso en mi diccionario.*	*No en-KWEN-troh EH-soh en mee deek-see-oh-NAH-ree-oh.*
Give me one anyway.	*Déme uno de todos modos.*	*DAY-may OO-noh day TOE-dohs MOE-dohs.*
No lettuce, for God's sake!	*¡Por Dios! ¡Sin lechuga!*	*Pohr DEE-ohs! Seen lay-CHOO-gah!*
Can't you see I'm a gringo?	*¿Qué no ve que soy gringo?*	*Kay no vay kay soy GREEN-go?*

DAILY LIFE 🏃

PERFECTING THE HAGGLE

Merchants and vendors will think you're a fool if you pay their asking price. The markup for Yankees is roughly five times an asking price that is already doubled for locals.

Even with this 1,000% markup, many things will still seem reasonably priced. Remember, though, that *you represent gringos and gringoland*. If you don't haggle, you'll make us all look thick.

These look well-made/delicious/Martian.	*Estos parecen estar bien hechos/ser deliciosos/ser Marcianos.*	*EHS-tohs pah-RAY-sen ehs-TAHR bee-EN AY-chos / sair day-lee-see-OH-sohs / sair Mar-see-AH-nohs.*
How much for one/two/half a kilo?	*¿Cuánto por uno/dos/medio kilo?*	*KWAN-toh por OO-noh / dohs / MAY-dee-oh KEE-loh?*
Nine cents! Ridiculous!	*¡Quinientos pesos! ¡Ridículo!*	*Keen-ee-YEN-tohs PAY-sohs! Ree-DEE-koo-loh!*
If I had money like that, I would be vacationing in France.	*Si tuviera ese dinero, estaría de vacaciones en Francia.*	*See too-vee-AIR-ah EH-say dee-NAIR-oh, ess-tar-EE-ah day vah-kah-see-OH-nays en FRAHN-see-ah.*

Would you consider three cents?	*¿Consideraría trescientos centavos?*	*Kohn-see-dair-ahr-EE-ah tray-see-EN-tohs sen-TAH-vohs?*
No need for shouting.	*No hay necesidad de gritar.*	*No eye nay-say-see-DAHD day gree-TAR.*
I'll buy it next door. Good-bye.	*Lo compro aquí al lado. Hasta luego.*	*Lo COM-pro ah-KEE ahl LAH-doh. AH-sta loo-AY-goh.*
That's more like it.	*Así está mejor.*	*Ah-SEE ehs-TAH may-HOAR.*
Done. Thank you, madam.	*Hecho. Muchas gracias, señora.*	*AY-choh. MOO-chahs GRA-see-ahs, seen-YORE-ah.*
I'm thrilled to have saved four cents.	*Estoy encantado de haber ahorrado doscientos centavos.*	*Ehs-TOY en-kahn-TAH-doh day ah-BAIR ah-or-RAH-doh dohs-see-EN-tohs sen-TAH-vohs.*

POST WASTE

Hot offices and low pay ensure long lines and inefficient postal service. And on occasion, stamps are removed from letters—especially from goofy postcards—and sold again. Avoiding this hazard is simple: send letters *registrado*. The stamps will be canceled right in front of you.

I'd like to send this airmail to the United States.	*Quisiera mandar esto vía aérea a Estados Unidos.*	*Kee-see-AIR-ah man-DAR EHS-toh VEE-ah ah-AIR-ee-ah ah ehs-TAH-dohs oo-NEED-ohs.*
Am I in time for the evening mule?	*¿Llegué a tiempo para la mula de la tarde?*	*Yeh-GAY ah tee-EM-poh PAR-ah la MOOL-ah day la TAR-day?*
Will it arrive by the turn of the century?	*¿Llegará a fin de siglo?*	*Yeh-gahr-AH ah feen day SEE-gloh?*
No guarantees?	*¿Sin garantías ?*	*Seen gah-rahn-TEE-ahs?*
Actually, sending letters into the Void is one of my hobbies.	*En realidad, mandar cartas al Vacío es uno de mis pasatiempos.*	*En ray-ahl-ee-DAHD, man-DAR CAR-tahs ahl vahs-EE-oh ehs OO-noh day meece pah-sah-tee-EM-pohs.*

DAILY LIFE

ESSENTIAL EXPLETIVES

Although Wicked Travelers invariably know a few curses, they almost never need to use them. If you must curse a native, do so under your breath or on a very long-distance call — some Latinos feel obligated to kill people who question their honor.

What whoreness!	*¡Qué putada!*	*Kay poo-TAH-dah!*
Don't mess with me, tostada-face!	*¡No me friegues, cara de tostada!*	*No may free-AY-gayss, KAH-rah day toast-AH-dah!*
Watch it, you with the wife who gets around!	*¡Cuídate, cabrón!*	*KWEE-dah-tay, cah-BRONE!*
I'll grind you into little sausages.	*Te voy a picar en pedacitos de salchicha.*	*Tay voy ah pee-KAR en pay-dah-SEE-tohss day sahl-CHEE-chah.*
And feed them to your mother.	*Y dárselos de comer a tu madre.*	*Ee DAHR-say-lohs day coh-MAIR ah too MAH-dray.*

EL BANCO DE QUIXOTE

A bank's machine-gun-toting guards are not there to prevent robberies; their job is to keep frustrated customers from killing sluggish clerks and each other.

Getting angry won't speed up the service, and patience is often just as pointless. Vitriol at least makes us feel better.

Sir, let me warn you.	*Señor, déjeme advertirle.*	*Seen-YOHR, DAY-heh-meh ad-ver-TEER-leh.*
I've been waiting for half an hour.	*Llevo esperando media hora.*	*YE-voh ess-pair-AHN-doh MAY-dee-ah OR-ah.*
Cut in front of me and you're a dead man.	*Cuélese y lo mato.*	*KWAY-lay-say ee loh MAH-toh.*
Ladies. Excuse me for interrupting your fascinating chat.	*Señoritas. Discúlpenme por interrumpir su plática tan interesante.*	*SEE-nyoh-REE-tahs. Dees-KOOL-pen-may pohr een-tair-oom-PEER soo PLAH-tee-kah tan een-tair-ehs-AHN-tay.*

📖 *DAILY LIFE*

I'd like to exchange some dollars.	*Quisiera cambiar unos dólares.*	Kee-see-AIR-ah kahm-bee-AHR OO-nohs doh-LAR-ehs.
Oh, no! Don't send me to window seven!	*¡Oh, no! ¡No me mande a la ventanilla siete!*	Oh, no! No may MAN-day ah lah ven-tah-NEE-yah see-ET-ay!
I know perfectly well there is no window seven!	*¡Sé muy bien que no existe la ventanilla siete!*	Say MOO-ee bee-EN kay no eks-EES-tay lah ven-tah-NEE-yah see-ET-ay!
Don't point that machine gun at me!	*¡No me apunte esa ametralla-dora!*	No may ah-POON-tay con eh-sah ah-meh-tra-ya-DOH-ra!
Are you fools?	*¿Están locos?*	Ehs-TAN LOH-kohs?
Can't you see this is a good deal?	*¿No ven que esto es un buen trato?*	No ven kay ESS-toh ehs oon bwain TRAH-toh?
I'm offering you dollars for pesos!	*¡Les estoy ofreciendo dólares por pesos!*	Lay ehs-TOY oh-fray-see-EN-doh doh-LAR-ehs pohr PEH-sohs!

BANISHING THE MINIATURE HUCKSTER

Even hardened North Americans are shocked at the poverty in the Hispanic world, where not all hucksters are adults, and some are actually cute. For those who cannot ignore importunate children, the following phrases are provided.

How old are you?	¿Qué edad tienes?	Kay ay-DAHD tee-EN-ehs?
Three is too young to be working.	Tres es muy chico para estar trabajando.	Trehs ehs MOO-ee CHEE-koh PAR-ah es-TAR trah-bah-HAN-doh.
Especially at midnight in a bar.	Sobre todo, en un bar a la medianoche.	SO-bray TOH-doh, en oon bar ah la MAY-dee-ah-NOH-chay.
Well, I don't need any Chiclets/dolls/rugs.	Bueno, no necesito Chicles/muñecas/alfombras.	BWAY-noh, no nay-say-see-toh CHEE-klayss / moon-YEK-ahs / ahl-FOAM-brahs.

🔖 DAILY LIFE

Look. Things are tough all over, kid.	*Mira chavo. Las cosas están duras en todas partes.*	*MEER-ah CHAH-voh. Las CO-sahs ehs-TAN DOO-rahs en TOH-dahs PAHR-tayss.*
Okay, okay. Here's thirty cents.	*Okay, okay. Aquí tienes doscientos centavos.*	*Oh-kay, oh-kay. Ah-KEE tee-EN-ayss doh-see-YEN-tohs sen-TAH-vohs.*
Go buy yourself a condo.	*Ve y cómprate un condominio.*	*Vay ee KOM-prah-tay oon kohn-doh-MEE-nee-oh.*

DAILY LIFE 🕵️

REPORTING THEFTS

There are only two reasons to request a police report: to get a vacation souvenir and for insurance purposes. If the police don't have to get out of their chairs, they may spend a few minutes on your case.

I'd like to report a mugging/ burglary/ pickpocket/ car theft.	*Quisiera denunciar un asalto/robo/ carterista/ robo de auto.*	*Kee-see-AIR-ah day-noon-see-AHR oon ah-sal-TOH / ROH-boh / cahr-ter-EES-tah / ROH-boh day ow-toh. Ess-PAIR-ay!*
Wait! Let me explain, please.	*¡Espere! Déjeme explicar, por favor.*	*Ess-PAIR-ay! DAY-hay-may eks-plee-KAHR, pohr fah-VOAR.*
I don't expect you to solve the crime.	*No espero que resuelva el crimen.*	*No ess-PAIR-oh kay race-WELL-vah el KREE-men.*
I do not expect to see my camera/ passport/money/ car again.	*No espero ver mi cámara/ pasaporte/dinero/ auto de nuevo.*	*No ess-PAIR-oh vair mee CAM-ar-ah / pah-sah-POHR-tay / dee-NAIR-oh / ow-toh day NWAY-voh.*

🛍 DAILY LIFE

All I need is a piece of paper from you.	*Lo único que necesito de usted es un papel.*	*Loh OO-nee-coh kay nay-say-SEE-toh day oos-TED ehs oon pah-PELL.*
It is for the insurance company.	*Es para la compañía de seguros.*	*Ehs PAR-ah lah kohm-pan-YEE-ah day say-GOOR-ohs.*
Here is a little something for your trouble.	*Aquí tiene algo por su molestia.*	*Ah-KEE tee-EN-ay AHL-go pohr soo moh-LESS-tee-ah.*
That's okay. Don't get up.	*Está bien. No se levante.*	*Ehs-TA bee-EN. No seh lay-VAHN-tay.*
Thank you for your kind attention, sir.	*Gracias por su amable atención, señor.*	*GRAH-see-ahs pohr soo ahm-AH-blay ah-ten-see-OHN, seen-yohr.*

CULTURE

THE ETERNAL SIESTA

Spend one day in a hot, dry country and you'll begin to understand why nothing gets done between noon and three o'clock. You may even wonder how anything ever gets done.

But you may also begin to understand the many wonderful meanings of the siesta tradition.

The clerk is taking a vertical siesta.	*El empleado está tomando una siesta parado.*	*El em-play-AH-doh ehs-TAH toh-MAHN-doh OO-nah see-ES-tah pah-RAH-doh.*
Our maid is on a permanent siesta.	*Nuestra sirvienta está en siesta permanente.*	*NWAY-strah seer-vee-EN-tah ehs-TAH en see-ES-tah pair-ma-NEN-tay.*
Excuse me, beautiful. Would you join me for a siesta?	*Disculpa, guapa. ¿Quisieras acompañarme a una siesta?*	*Dees-KOOL-pah, GWAH-pah. Kee-see-AIR-ahs ah-comb-pahn-YAR-may ah OO-nah see-EST-ah?*

CULTURE

MAÑANA COUNTERATTACK

There is no way to avoid frustration with the Latin lack of urgency. But we can turn the tables now and then.

Yes, we're leaving.	*Sí, nos vamos.*	*See, nohss BAH-mohss.*
We had a wonderful time.	*La pasamos muy bien.*	*La pah-SAH-mos MOO-ee bee-EN.*
We like you very much.	*Nos cae muy bien.*	*Nohs CAH-eh moo-ee bee-EN.*
Pay the bill?	*¿Pagar la cuenta?*	*Pah-GAHR la KWEN-tah?*
Hey, what's the hurry?	*Oiga, ¿cuál es la prisa?*	*OY-gah, KWAL ehs la PREE-sah?*
Aren't we friends?	*¿Que no somos amigos?*	*Kay no SO-mohss ah-MEE-gohs?*
Did you hurry for us?	*¿Acaso se apuró por nosotros?*	*Ah-CAH-soh say ah-poo-ROH pohr no-SO-trohss?*
We'll pay tomorrow!	*¡Le pagaremos mañana!*	*Lay pah-gah-RAY-mohss man-YAH-nah!*

EL BUSINESS MEETING

Business practices are different in the Spanish-speaking world. Conversations may be held at close range; even if you can see the pores on your associate's nose, you must not back away. This would be a serious loss of face. Likewise, you must hold eye contact like a gunfighter.

Latin businessmen are more comfortable with physical contact. If your counterpart squeezes your shoulders or fondles your lapels, do not be alarmed. He is probably just lonely.

Good afternoon, Mr. Honorable Senior Vice President Estrada.	*Buenas tardes, honorable señor vicepresidente ejecutivo Estrada.*	*BWAY-nahs TAR-dayss, ohn-or-AH-bleh seen-YOHR veece-pray-see-DEN-tay eh-hay-koo-TEE-voh Ehs-TRAH-dah.*
I have brought you some gifts.	*Le he traído unos regalos.*	*Lay ay try-EE-doh OO-nohs ray-GAH-los.*
This is a pen. This is a pencil.	*Esto es una pluma. Esto es un lápiz.*	*EHS-toh ehs OO-nah PLOO-mah. EHS-toh ehs OON LAH-peece.*
Do you like our company logo?	*¿Le gusta el logotipo de nuestra compañía?*	*Lay GOO-stah el loh-go-TEEP-oh day NWACE-trah kohm-pahn-YEE-ah?*

🎉 CULTURE

You didn't have to get me a gift!	¡No tenía usted que regalarme nada!	No ten-EE-ah oos-TED kay ray-gah-LAR-may NAH-dah!
Well, if you insist.	Bueno, si insiste.	BWAY-noh, see een-SEES-tay.
This is a fine ashtray. Such sturdy plastic!	Es un cenicero fino. ¡Un plástico tan resistente!	Ehs oon seh-nee-SEH-ro FEEN-oh. Oon PLAH-steek-oh tahn ray-zees-TEN-tay!
Go ahead! Try your new pen!	¡Ande! ¡Pruebe su pluma nueva!	AHN-day! Proo-AY-bay soo PLOO-mah NWAY-vah!
Sign on this line, Your Excellency!	¡Firme aquí, Su Excelencia!	FEER-may ah-KEE, soo ex-cell-EN-see-ah!

CULTURE

LA REVOLUTION

If you are captured by revolutionaries, accept the fact that they are serious. Even if they speak in reverent tones about Mao Tse-tung, do not laugh. Just play along and hope somebody pays your ransom.

Brothers and sisters of the revolution!	*¡Hermanos y hermanas de la revolución!*	*Air-MAHN-ohs ee air-MAHN-ahs day la rev-oh-loo-see-OHN!*
I believe in your cause, whatever it is.	*Creo en su causa, sea cual sea.*	*KRAY-oh en soo COW-sah, SAY-ah KWAL SAY-ah.*
Down with imperialism/ colonialism/ capitalism!	*¡Abajo con el imperialismo/ colonialismo/ capitalismo!*	*Ah-BAH-ho con el eem-per-ee-ahl-EEZ-moh / coh-lohn-ee-ahl-EEZ-moh / cah-pee-tahl-EEZ-moh!*
Take my MasterCard!	*¡Tome mi tarjeta de crédito!*	*TOH-may mee tar-HAY-tah day CRAY-dee-toh!*
Buy yourselves some boots/ uniforms/sun-glasses!	*¡Cómprense unas botas/ uniformes/ anteojos oscuros!*	*COMB-pren-say OO-nahs BOAT-ahs / oo-nee-FOR-mayss / an-teh OH-hos os-KOO-ros!*

CULTURE

HANDY GUIDE TO LATIN REVOLUTIONARIES

COUNTRY/ NAME	GOAL	LIKES	DISLIKES
Colombia/ FARC	Freedom for Drug Dealers	Julio Iglesias Small bills Rocket launchers	Extradition Vanilla Ice Brooks Brothers
Nicaragua/ Contras	Recover Mercedes Dealerships	Miami real estate "Humanitarian Aid" Interrogating nuns	Schools Hospitals Voters
Peru/ Shining Path	Maoist Government	Coca leaves Coca paste Staying up late	Capitalism Democracy Holding jobs
Puerto Rico/ FALN	Puerto Rican Nationhood	U.S. food stamps U.S. dollars Plastic explosives	Actual danger "Gilligan's Island"
Spain/ ETA	Basque Independence	Jai-Alai Spicy fish sauces Killing policemen	Spanish French Paying taxes

CULTURE 🍴

LOVE IN THE TIME OF SEVERE ABDOMINAL CRAMPS

A sophisticated traveler is able to woo a native on his/her own turf and in her own tongue. But special phrases are needed to deal with the unique challenges of a Latin love affair.

Ai.	*Ai.*	*Ai.*
You make me hot, my chili pepper.	*Me calientas mucho, chilito mío.*	*May cah-lee-EN-tahs MOO-choh, chee-LEE-toh MEE-oh.*
Am I in heaven or in hell?	*¿Estoy en el cielo o en el infierno?*	*Es-TOY en el see-AY-loh oh en el een-fee-AIR-noh?*
If you love me, my little refried bean, fetch the thermometer.	*Si me amas, mi frijolito refrito, traime el termómetro.*	*See may AH-mas, mee free-ho-LEE-toh ray-FREE-toh, tra-EE-meh el ter-MOH-may-troh.*
Yes. As I suspected.	*Sí. Como lo sospechaba.*	*See. COH-moh loh soas-pay-CHAH-bah.*
One hundred four and a half degrees.	*Ciento cuatro y medio grados.*	*See-EHN-toh KWA-troh ee MEH-dee-oh GRAH-dohs.*

🍭 *CULTURE*

I am near death.	*Estoy cerca de la muerte.*	*Ess-TOY SAIR-kah day la MWER-tay.*
Love me but once more before I die, my little empanada.	*Amame una última vez antes de que me muera, mi pequeña empanada.*	*AH-mah-may OO-nah OOL-tee-mah vase ahn-tes day kay may MWAIR-ah, mee pay-KAIN-yah em-pah-NAH-dah.*
Wait! Holy Mother of God!	*¡Espera! ¡Santa Madre de Dios!*	*Ess-PAIR-ah! SAHN-tah MAH-dray day dee-OHS!*
I must get back to the bathroom!	*¡Tengo que volver al baño!*	*TEN-go kay vohl-VAIR ahl BAHN-yoh!*

CULTURE 🎺

COCKFIGHTS

Among many rural people,
cockfighting is honorable
and just. They know how mean these birds really
are and figure the bastards have it coming.

The contests are not inherently interesting, so
everybody bets on which bird will survive.

The cock was not brave/fierce/lucky.	*El gallo no fue valiente/bravo/afortunado.*	*El GAHL-yoh no foo-eh vah-lee-EN-tay / BRAH-voh / ah-for-too-NAH-do.*
He lost 10,000 pesos for me.	*Me hizo perder diez mil pesos.*	*May EE-soh pair-DAIR dee-ACE meel PAY-sohs.*
He had the fortitude of mozzarella.	*Tuvo la fortaleza de la mozzarella.*	*TOO-voh la for-tah-LAY-sah day la moat-sah-RAY-lah.*
And the heart of a parakeet.	*Y el corazón de un perico.*	*Ee el kohr-ah-SOHN day oon pair-EE-coh.*
Now his stud days are finished.	*Ahora sus días de semental han acabado.*	*Ah-OR-ah sooce DEE-ahs day sem-en-TAHL ahn ah-kah-BAH-doh.*

BULLFIGHTS

Among aficionados, bullfighting is more art than sport, more poetry than cruelty. You can take comfort in the knowledge that the bull sometimes wins. If you want to be accepted in machismo company, toss around a few of the following phrases.

The picador is a villain!	*¡El picador es un villano!*	*El pee-kah-DOOR ehs oon vee-YAH-noh!*
The bull, he is handsome.	*El toro es guapo.*	*El TOH-roh ehs GWA-poh.*
He moves like a thundercloud across the landscape.	*Se mueve como un nubarrón por el campo.*	*Say MWAY-vay COH-moh oon noo-bahr-ROHN pore el CAHM-poh.*
His thing is like a tree trunk.	*Su asunto es como un tronco de árbol.*	*Soo ah-SOON-toh ehs COH-moh oon TRON-koh day AR-bohl.*
His brain is like a pinto bean.	*Su cerebro es como un frijol bayo.*	*Soo sair-RAY-broh ehs COH-moh oon free-HOLE BY-yoh.*

CULTURE 🎺

MARIACHI AT A DISTANCE

The joys of mariachi are elusive and mysterious. Yet we are endlessly subjected to the music by the well-meaning players who circumnavigate dining rooms like huge germs in sombreros. A few phrases can help us keep the players at a distance.

Hey! High-ya!	*¡RRRijajai!*	*RRReee-HI-HI!*
What loud costumes you have!	*¡Qué trajes tan llamativos!*	*Kay TRAH-hayss tahn yah-mah-TEE-vohs!*
What forceful/ energetic/familiar music!	*¡Qué música tan fuerte/enérgica/ familiar!*	*Kay MOO-see-kah tahn FWER-tay / eh-NEHR-hee-kah / fah-meel-ee-AR!*
It's a lot of fun.	*Es tan divertida.*	*Ehs tahn dee-vair-TEE-dah.*
Now please get your maracas out of my face.	*Ahora por favor saque esas maracas de mi cara.*	*Ah-OR-ah pohr-fah-VOAR SAH-keh EH-sahs mah-RAHK-ahs day mee CAH-rah.*
I am trying to eat.	*Estoy tratando de comer.*	*Ess-TOY trah-TAHN-doh day coh-MAIR.*

THE POLITE GUEST'S GUIDE TO ENTRÉE INDENTIFICATION

People south of the border eat many animals not found in barnyards. When invited to dine in a native's home, your chances of being served something new and mysterious are therefore high.

When you receive your food, examine the sauce and then discreetly clear some away from a corner of the item in question. Note its color and texture and cut into it, noting toughness, internal features, and squirting or oozing. Then take a small bite and consider how it compares to more familiar food.

Meat	Spanish Name	Characteristics	Comments
agouti	tepescuintle	gamey, pork-like	large rodent
armadillo	armadillo	gamey, agouti-like	may be road kill
Chihuahua	itzcuintli	tiny claws	special delicacy
goat	cabrito	unusually greasy	tasty if young
lizard	iguana	chicken-like	another edible pet
turtle	tortuga	juicy, steak-like	endangered species
worm	gusano	worm-like	deep-fried, crunchy

THE MODEL GUEST ✳

NATIVES AT HOME

If you are invited to a local home for dinner, arrive about two hours late. Once the conversation begins, choose non-controversial subjects. Your host may feel compelled to defend the honor of his ancestors, his country, his wife, and her cooking skills.

Good to see you at last, General and Mrs. Hernández.	*Qué bueno verlos finalmente General y Señora Hernández.*	*Kay BWAY-noh VAIR-loh fee-nahl-MEN-tay hen-air-AHL ee seen-YOAR-ah hair-NAN-dez.*
Your apartment/ house is magnificent.	*Su apartamento/ casa es magnífico(a).*	*Soo ah-par-ta-MEN-toh / CAH-sah ehs mag-NEEF-ee-coh(cah).*
The heavy wooden/leather furniture is fine and austere.	*Los muebles de madera/cuero son finos y austeros.*	*Lohs MWAY-blayss day mah-DAIR-ah / KWAIR-oh sohn FEEN-ohs ee aust-AIR-ohs.*
The gold wall-paper is equally attractive.	*El empapelado dorado es igualmente atractivo.*	*El em-pah-pay-LAH-doh doh-RAH-doh ehs ee-gwal-MEN-tay ah-trahk-TEE-voh.*

That was the best meal I've ever had after midnight.	*Esa es la mejor cena que he comido después de medianoche.*	*EHS-ah ehs la may-HORE SEH-nah kay ay co-MEE-doh dess-PWEHS day MAY-dee-ah NOH-chay.*
I'm so stuffed I don't think I have room for flan.	*Estoy tan lleno que no creo tener espacio para el flan.*	*EHS-toy tahn YAY-noh no CRAY-oh ten-AIR ess-PASS-ee-oh PAR-ah el flahn.*
No need for threats, General!	*¡No hay necesidad de amenazas, General!*	*No ay nay-SAY-see-DAHD day ah-meh-NAH-sahss, hen-air-AHL!*
Of course I'll have some!	*¡Claro que probaré un pedazo!*	*KLAR-oh kay pro-bar-AY oon pay-DAH-soh!*

THE MODEL GUEST ✳

THE INEVITABLE THANK-YOU NOTE

The thank-you note is fast becoming a lost art, but it is still expected among civilized people. A simple card can smooth ruffled feathers and lead to fresh invitations.

Dear General Hernández,	*Estimado General Hernández,*
Thank you for the wonderful evening.	*Gracias por una agradable velada.*
That liquor was certainly strong!	*¡Aquel licor era realmente fuerte!*
I am sorry I mentioned politics/your wife's enormity.	*Siento haber hablado de política/del tamaño de su esposa.*
I admire military rule/300-pound women.	*Admiro el gobierno militar/mujeres de 140 kilos.*
As a matter of fact, my own beloved wife is a dictator/orangutan.	*En realidad, mi propia esposa querida es una dictadora/orangután.*
Thank you for canceling the death squad/duel at dawn.	*Gracias por cancelar el escuadrón de fusilamiento/duelo al amanecer.*
Best regards,	*Saludos,*

¿? HELP

GRINGO-MATIC™ EMERGENCY DICTIONARY

attorney	*abogado*	*ah-boh-GAH-doh*
bacteria	*bacterias*	*bahk-TEH-ree-ahss*
bathroom	*baño*	*BAHN-yo*
bribe	*soborno*	*so-BOHR-noh*
cramps	*cólicos*	*KOH-lee-kohss*
death	*muerte*	*MWER-tay*
dysentary	*disenteria*	*diss-en-tair-EE-ah*
embassy	*embajada*	*em-bah-HAH-dah*
innocent	*inocente*	*een-oh-SEN-tay*
pardon (as in judicial)	*indulto*	*een-DOOL-toh*
phone call	*llamada telefonica*	*yah-MAH-dah tell-ay-FON-ee-kah*
rights (as in human)	*derechos*	*deh-RAY-chohss*
scorpion	*alacrán*	*ah-lah-KRAHN*

HELP ¿?

GRINGO-MATIC™ QUICK REFERENCE

I like.	Me gusta.	May GOOS-tah.
I don't like.	No me gusta.	No may GOOS-tah.
I want this.	Quiero esto.	Key-AIR-oh EHS-toh.
I want that.	Quiero aquello.	Key-AIR-oh ah-KAY-oh.
I want everything.	Lo quiero todo.	Loh key-AIR-oh TOH-doh.
Not tomorrow.	Mañana no.	Mahn-YAHN-ah no.
Now.	Ahora.	Ah-OR-ah.
How much does it cost?	¿Cuánto cuesta?	KWAHN-toh KWES-tah?
Where is the toilet?	¿Dónde está el baño?	DON-day es-TAH el BAHN-yoh?
How do I get out of here?	¿Cómo salgo de aquí?	COH-moh SAHL-goh day ah-KEE?